Bruno Schlesinger
1911-2010

◆

A Life
in Letters & Learning

Contributors
- Mary Griffin Burns
- Nancy Fallon
- Philip Gleason
- Gail Porter Mandell
- Patricia Ferris McGinn
- Thomas Merton
- Marvin R. O'Connell
- Bruno P. Schlesinger
- Thomas Schlesinger

**Printed in the United States of America
Font throughout text is Garamond.**

Word cloud generated at www.Wordle.com

Copies available at Lulu.com & Amazon.com

For further information, please contact
Rick Regan
PO Box 40039
Raleigh, NC 27629
rick@rickregan.net

ISBN: 978-1493584086

For Bruno, from whom so many learned so much.

Foreword

Philip Gleason

At Notre Dame, they were called the "Foreign Legion" or the "Department of Fractured English." Such a group existed at many other Catholic colleges, for they too harbored refugee scholars who fled Europe in the 1930s and 40s. Nor did the facetious labels mean that these men (and virtually all were men) were unappreciated, for their positive contribution to the academic quality of the places where they taught was unmistakable.

The full impact of this influx of transplanted Europeans on the whole broad spectrum of American higher education has never been adequately assessed. Among Catholic institutions even their presence is all but unknown. Nearly all of them have now passed from the scene. The distinguished Hungarian-born historian, John Lukacs – who began his American career at Philadelphia's Chestnut Hill College in 1947 – is still active, but there cannot be many more.

Among the longest-lived was **Bruno Schlesinger**, my friend of fifty years and more, who died in 2010, five years after retiring from a six-decade teaching career at Notre Dame's sister institution, Saint Mary's College. This is his story.

Bruno's escape from Nazism illuminates the human drama experienced by these refugee intellectuals. His career in the United States is distinctive in that he made his academic mark, not in the form of books and articles, but by way of a curricular innovation that opened new intellectual vistas for hundreds of young women beginning in 1956 and extending to the present.

Table of Contents

From Vienna to South Bend: A Refugee Professor's Story

Philip Gleason[1]

Appeared first in <u>American Catholic Studies,</u> vol. 124, No. 2 (Summer 2013), pp. 71-85, and is reprinted here, with minor stylistic changes, and with the permission of the editors.

Bruno P. Schlesinger (1911-2010), one of the many refugee intellectuals and scholars who fled from Nazism in the 1930s, taught for sixty years at Saint Mary's College, Notre Dame, Indiana. This sketch of his life story and professional career honors his personal contribution to American Catholic higher education and at the same time calls attention to a topic worthy of much more research – the role played by these refugees in the development of American Catholic intellectual life in the mid-twentieth century.

Austria and Escape from the Nazis

Bruno P. Schlesinger was born in 1911 in Neunkirchen, a small

Austrian town some forty miles south of Vienna. The family was Jewish. His father, Max, ran motorcycle/bicycle sales and repair shop, on the second floor of which Bruno and a younger brother, Kurt, lived with their parents. His education began at the local Volkschule; after that he moved on to a Gymnasium in Wiener-Neustadt, a larger city near Vienna. Upon completing his secondary studies, Bruno spent two years at the German School of Drama in Munich, where, according to one report, he supported himself by playing the piano in a cabaret. Evidently his theatrical aspirations didn't work out, for in 1933 he returned to Austria and enrolled at the University of Vienna, pursuing studies in law and political science.

---

1 Philip Gleason, professor of history emeritus at the University of Notre Dame, is a past president of the American Catholic Historical Association and author of a number of books and articles on American Catholic history.

L to R: Dr. Walter Bauer, Fr. Leopold Ungar & Bruno Schlesinger. ca. mid-1930s

It was during his five years at the university that Bruno became a Catholic. To my knowledge, he never told anyone the story of his conversion, but the family is convinced that Father John Oesterreicher – himself a Jewish convert then active in Vienna and only a few years older than Bruno – was centrally involved. Indeed, it was at a Bible study group organized by Oesterreicher that Bruno met Alice Teweles, a student at Vienna's Academy of Fine Art, who was to become his wife. Surviving correspondence from a later date establishes that Bruno and Oesterreicher – by then "Monsignor" and founder of the Institute of Judaeo-Christian Studies at Seton Hall University – remained close friends. That friendship played a role in Bruno's escape from Austria after German troops seized control of the country in March of 1938.

He had not yet completed his university studies at the time of the so-called *Anschluss*, the occupation and annexation of Austria into Nazi Germany in March 1938, but despite being Jewish by "race," Bruno did not attract hostile attention for the first few months of the new Nazi regime. That changed in the summer of 1938 when he was picked up and interrogated by the Gestapo at the Hotel Metropol, their Viennese headquarters. He was released later the same day, but the experience – plus the fact that one of his uncles had already been sent to a concentration camp – convinced Bruno that he could no longer remain in Austria. His brother,

Kurt, had already gotten out; his parents, however, could not bring themselves to leave. About a year and a half later they too were sent to a concentration camp where, as Bruno put it in a three-page memoir written in his old age, they "disappeared without a trace."

Dr. Walter Bauer & Bruno Schlesinger ca. 1938

After adding his name to a waiting list for an American visa, Bruno decided to put some distance between himself and the Nazis by departing for Yugoslavia, for which he did get a visa. His parents, along with Alice and her stepmother, saw him off at the railroad station sometime in the late summer or early fall of 1938.

After an indeterminate, but brief, stay in Yugoslavia, Bruno traveled to Switzerland on a short-term entry permit. At this point the sources differ in detail. In his previously mentioned memoir, Bruno says only that despite lacking entry papers for France, he was persuaded to make a foolish attempt to walk across the Swiss-French border in broad daylight. According to his daughter, Mary, to whom he told the story as they traveled together through the same territory many years later, he was victimized by a con man who demanded payment for recommending a course of action so brazenly obvious it was sure to succeed. To complicate matters further, Kurt, then in Paris, may have contacted the coyote in good faith, asking him to help Bruno enter France.

Whatever the immediate background, Bruno embarked on his quixotic border-crossing on October 27, 1938. He was promptly arrested for illegal entry and held by the French police in

Mulhouse. Brought before a magistrate a few days later, he was sentenced to spend a month in jail and pay a fine of 100 francs. He later recalled that his fellow inmates were pickpockets and other small time crooks, and that boredom was the most disagreeable feature of his incarceration. Even that was broken up, according to his memoir, by the visit of a "friendly gentleman" who suggested that he join the French Foreign Legion – advice Bruno declined.

In the meantime, Father Oesterreicher – now himself a refugee in Paris – almost certainly inspired an appeal on Bruno's behalf by Charles Devaux, a French priest active in missionary work with Jews, who aided many fugitives from Nazism. Father Devaux assured the authorities in Mulhouse that Bruno had friends in Paris who vouched for him and would provide for his needs while he waited for his American visa to be processed. It is unclear whether this intervention was decisive, but on November 24th Bruno was released from prison and ordered to leave France within fifteen days.

Three friends in Vienna, mid-1930s.

Unlike Father John Oesterreicher at left, & Bruno Schlesinger at right,

friend Hans Zimmerl, center, remained in Austria and was later executed by the Nazis.

A Life in Learning & Letters

That deadline could, however, be extended on appeal; after he too reached Paris, Bruno was able to get it renewed through the early months of 1939. His clerical connections had by that time procured assistance at the American end of things. As early as December 5, 1938, the superior of a Benedictine community in New Jersey forwarded to immigration authorities the necessary certification that Bruno – "a close friend of members of our Benedictine Order in Austria" – was of good character and would not become a public charge in the United States. With continuing assistance from friends in Paris, his visa came through in the late winter or early spring of 1939.

Leaving Kurt and Father Oesterreicher behind, Bruno crossed the Atlantic on the Aquitania, arriving in New York toward the end of May. As the ship made its way into the harbor, he confesses to being so absorbed in gazing at the city's forest of skyscrapers that he missed seeing the Statue of Liberty.

Early Years in America

Little is known about Bruno's stay in New York. Years later, in speaking to a Saint Mary's alumnae group, he reported seeing many movies to improve his English, but said nothing about where he lived, how he supported himself, or how long he remained in the city. Kurt, who left Paris after Bruno, also reached New York during this period. But the high point of Bruno's sojourn there was Alice's arrival.

Unfortunately the story of Alice's escape from Austria is even sketchier than Bruno's. But because her father was Jewish, it would have been perilous for her to remain there, and since she and Bruno were in a deeply committed relationship, if not actually engaged, it is reasonable to assume that, though they fled Austria separately, they planned to meet again in the United States. The plausibility of that supposition is reinforced by the fact that on September 8, 1938 – just as Bruno was leaving, or preparing to leave, Vienna – a well-to-do aunt in California certified to immigration authorities that her niece, Alice Teweles, would not become a public charge if permitted to enter the United States.

Bruno and Alice celebrated their reunion with visits to the Metropolitan Museum of Art and other cultural monuments (including the New York World's Fair in Flushing Meadows). However, the prospect of familial support in California seemed to offer the most promising future. As Bruno told the story at the alumnae gathering, he and Alice crossed the country by train, probably in the late summer of 1939. However, the reception awaiting them in Whittier – the aunt's residence – was notably lacking in enthusiasm. Their hostess had not, after all, anticipated providing shelter for three refugees – for at this point Kurt reappears in the story, having made the cross-country trip on a bus.

Alice Teweles & Bruno Schlesinger, ca. 1940

The resulting sequence of events is murky, but Bruno and Alice moved as soon as they could to Los Angeles. There they were married in May of 1940 – thus remedying what some of Alice's relatives regarded as scandalous cohabitation in separate rooms of the same house! Alice quickly found employment as a fashion illustrator at Bullock's, a department store in the city. Her talent provided the newly married couple's only consistent source of income as Bruno bounced from one unsatisfactory job to another over the next two years.

Bruno & Alice on their wedding day,

Los Angeles, May 27, 1940

Indeed, a review of his employment record puts one in mind of a Charlie Chaplin comedy. He was successively a door-to-door salesman of Fuller brushes; operator of an unprofitable soft drink and candy stand; soda jerk in a drug store; shipping clerk in a warehouse; and trimmer and sprinkler of lettuce at a supermarket called "Westwood Ho!" Interspersed among his various jobs were sporadic efforts at self-improvement: trade-school training as an electrician, and a university course in economics. None of this was really Bruno's métier. His vocational salvation, when it finally came about, was the result of his being an inveterate haunter of libraries and browser of periodicals.

While pursuing this avocation in the Los Angeles public library, Bruno's eye fell on the dark blue covers of *The Review of Politics*. Leafing through this journal, recently established at the University of Notre Dame and committed to probing the historical and philosophical dimensions of its subject, his excitement grew. Its founding editor, Waldemar Gurian, was himself an émigré and a Jewish convert to Catholicism who had earlier been involved in some of Father Oesterreicher's projects. The name of Jacques Maritain and other contributors to the *Review* were familiar to Bruno from his immersion in European Catholic intellectual life. Another feature of the journal must have seemed to him

16

providential – a notice in the back pages stating that Notre Dame offered a graduate program in politics and invited applications. This fortuitous discovery set in motion a series of events that Bruno regarded as having saved his life.

Graduate School Years

Bruno lost no time in sending a letter of inquiry to Notre Dame, receiving in reply an official application blank. Although he couldn't have provided the requested transcript of his academic record and letters of recommendation from his professors in Austria, Bruno was admitted to graduate school, promised financial assistance, and instructed to report for the beginning of Notre Dame's fall term in September, 1942. Shortly before that date, Bruno and Alice found an apartment in bustling wartime South Bend and began a life whose stability differed markedly from what they had known over the previous four years. For Alice that meant being able to combine her artistic work – as portraitist, illustrator of children's books, and designer of greeting cards – with her role as wife and (in time) mother of four children. For Bruno it meant earning a Ph. D. in political science and going on to a deeply rewarding career as a college professor.

By 1945 he had satisfied all the requirements for the doctorate except completion of a dissertation. Several factors delayed his getting over that hurdle. First, a teaching position had unexpectedly opened up at Saint Mary's when Otto von Simson, another refugee from Nazism and a leading historian of medieval art and architecture, was invited to join the faculty of the University of Chicago. Accepting the offer would mean breaking his contract at Saint Mary's unless he could find someone to take over his courses in mid-year. Von Simson, who knew Bruno well, recommended him as the necessary replacement. Saint Mary's accepted the arrangement, and Bruno began his career at the college on a one-semester contract – "gradually extended," as he wryly put it, "to sixty years."

Besides being delayed by his newly acquired teaching duties – primarily in history and art history – Bruno had some difficulty settling on a dissertation topic. He had originally hoped to write on either Max Weber (as I remember the story) or Jacob Burckhardt (as a colleague who knew him well remembers). In any case, he had been anticipated; another recent dissertation dealt with the subject in exactly the way he planned to approach it.

The final complication arose from tensions that developed with his academic mentor, Waldemar Gurian. The closest Bruno ever came to specifying the nature of the breach between them was to speak of Gurian's "craziness." For his part, Gurian regarded Bruno as "neurotic" and an ingrate. My own guess – and it is nothing more – is that Bruno did not display the degree of subservience Gurian thought his due as Herr Doktor Professor. Whatever the precise situation, Bruno managed to change dissertation directors while Gurian was away from Notre Dame on a leave of absence. His new mentor, Ferdinand A. Hermens, also a European émigré, was by contrast to Gurian notably sweet-tempered. That cleared away the last road block to Bruno's completing the dissertation, *Christopher Dawson and the Modern Political Crisis*. It was approved in 1949, and he got his degree that summer.

Despite Bruno's later enthusiasm for Christopher Dawson's educational ideas, his dissertation shows that he was by no means uncritical in his admiration for this giant of the Catholic intellectual revival of the interwar years. In analyzing the books Dawson had written on contemporary affairs in the early and middle 1930s, Bruno took note of his relatively benign interpretation of the rise of dictatorships in Italy and Germany (but not Russia), and the contrasting "sharply critical tone" he adopted in discussing the western democracies. The latter, Dawson saw as simply not as far along in the inevitable drift toward totalitarianism that resulted from the secularization of western culture and the progressive extension of state control over all aspects of human activity.

Bruno acknowledged that in works written during and after World War II, Dawson came to a clearer understanding of the true nature of totalitarianism. His failure to do so earlier, Bruno attributed to Dawson's lack of experience in politics and his inattention to political factors in shaping human events. That, in turn, could be linked to Dawson's concentration on religion as the key element in human history.

Although Dawson applied this perspective brilliantly in his large scale treatment of western civilization, it misled him into lumping liberal democracies together with totalitarian regimes as superficially different manifestations of the same underlying phenomenon. Bruno, who had first-hand experience of totalitarianism, knew Dawson had erred in this matter, but it did not diminish his respect for Dawson's achievement in books like *Progress and Religion* (1928), *The Making of Europe* (1932), and *Religion and the Rise of Western Culture* (1950).

Central to these books – and to all of Dawson's work—was his conviction that religion furnished the basic inspiration and animating force in all the great world cultures. Christianity played that role in the case of western culture. While giving full credit to the importance of Jewish, Greco-Roman, barbarian, and Moorish elements – and acknowledging the degree to which Christianity had lost its cultural hegemony in recent centuries – Dawson nevertheless insisted that western culture was at bottom Christian. From this it followed that the cultural crisis of the twentieth century could not be adequately understood unless analyzed in the light of western civilization's Christian heritage.

Dawson and the Background of Saint Mary's Program in Christian Culture

Shortly after the end of the World War II, Dawson began to expound the educational implications of his overall interpretation. The timing was propitious since his message resonated with two themes at the forefront of concern among American educators in the postwar years.

First, the widely prevailing sense of cultural crisis brought on by totalitarianism and war highlighted the need for an education that provided solid grounding for the values Americans regarded as the basis of their national existence.

A second theme centered on the need for curricular "integration," i.e., an approach that embodied a unifying principle enabling students to put together all they were learning in a meaningful way. Much had been written on this matter in the 1930s, but the war set off a new freshet of books and articles in which the need for curricular integration overlapped and merged together with deeper concern about the underlying crisis of the age.

Catholic educators fully shared these concerns. Indeed, they were almost obsessive on the subject of curricular integration. But since Scholastic philosophy was traditionally touted as performing this function, the relevance of Dawson's work went unnoticed until the publication of his article, "Education and Christian Culture" in the December 4, 1953, issue of *Commonweal*.

A Life in Learning & Letters

Here he argued that the study of Christian culture could serve as the unifying focus sadly lacking in American higher education which, after abandoning the traditional classical curriculum, had dissolved into "a chaos of competing specialisms." At the same time – and even more important – studying the evolution of Christian culture over time would acquaint students with the historic roots of the values and institutions that formed the bedrock of western civilization.

As a result of the interest stimulated by Dawson's article, a conference ostensibly devoted to "Christian Culture and Catholic Higher Education" brought together about a hundred Catholic educators at Notre Dame in the spring of 1955. Mercifully, Dawson was not present at this gathering, for his ideas got short shrift indeed. Only one speaker treated them extensively, and he was quite critical. Three simply ignored Dawson in favor of their own curricular hobby-horses. Two talked about matters only remotely relevant. The only speaker who expressed support for Dawson's approach was a classicist whose main concern was making sure that patristic writings weren't left out of any such curricular program.

The Early Years of the Christian Culture Program

For a true Dawsonian, the conference must have been a great disappointment. It likewise demonstrated that translating Dawson's ideas into an actual curricular program – and getting it accepted at even a Catholic college – was going to be an uphill battle. But Bruno, by this time deeply committed to Dawson's ideas, had great stores of determination and he pressed forward with an attempt to do just that at Saint Mary's. First, he presented an outline of his project to Sister Maria Renata, C.S.C., the chairperson of the history department of which he was a member. She, however, had no interest in a program that would obviously compete with history for students and administrative support. She simply tabled Bruno's proposal.

Stymied at the departmental level, Bruno took his sketch of a program in Christian culture directly to the president of Saint Mary's, Sister M. Madeleva, C.S.C. – a woman widely admired as an imaginative leader among Catholic educators. She, too, was slow to respond, no doubt weighing Sister Renata's objections. But thanks in part to encouragement from Frank Sheed, the highly respected Catholic publisher who knew and admired Bruno, she authorized

his curricular experiment to begin in the fall semester of 1956.

Bruno seems to have envisioned his proposal as a "pilot project" designed for eventual adoption on a college-wide basis – and, ideally, as a model for emulation by other institutions. What Sister Madeleva actually approved, and what the Christian Culture Program remained, was a tightly integrated interdisciplinary major, administratively distinct from the history department, that students could elect in their junior and senior years.

As worked out by Bruno in consultation with Dawson (who had high hopes for the experiment), the program focused on the relationship of "Christianity and Culture" in four historical epochs, to each of which a semester was devoted. The first covered the formative period from apostolic times to the twelfth century under the heading, "*The Making of Europe.*" That was followed by "*Medieval Christendom*," "*The Age of Religious Division*," and "*The Age of Revolutions and World Wars.*"

There were two main instructional tracks: a four-semester sequence of synthesizing lectures and assigned readings, taught by Bruno, which drew heavily on Dawson's ideas, and an accompanying series of colloquia, in which students discussed original texts from the period covered in the lectures. In the first semester, for example, St. Augustine's *Confessions* or his *City of God*, the *Rule of St. Benedict*, *The Song of Roland*, various Latin hymns, and examples of early Christian art were among the works discussed.

Christian Culture Symposium, 1960

L to R, seated: Mrs. Valery Dawson, Christopher Dawson, Sister M. Madeleva (president of Saint Mary's College), Bruno Schlesinger;

L to R, standing: Mircea Eliade (University of Chicago) and Vernon Bourke (St. Louis University)

Specialists from other departments at Saint Mary's, or from Notre Dame, sometimes led the colloquia or offered supplemental courses in philosophy, theology, or other subjects. In 1958 and 1959, for example, I taught a course on "Religion in American Culture" to second-semester seniors. Electives from other departments at Saint Mary's could be counted toward a Christian Culture degree, and some students combined Christian Culture with history, philosophy, or some other subject as a "double major."

A series of lectures by distinguished scholars, originally funded by grants from the Lilly Endowment of Indianapolis, added greatly to the éclat of the Christian Culture Program and enriched the intellectual life of the larger South Bend community. Dawson – who was in the United States from 1958 to 1962 as holder of a newly founded Chair of Roman Catholic Studies at Harvard – was one of the first Lilly lecturers. Others who appeared in the early years of the program included the poet, Louise Bogan; the historian of religion, Mircea Eliade; the medievalist, Giles Constable; Dante scholars, Francis Fergusson and John Freccero; Agnes Mongan, director of the Fogg Museum at Harvard; Alan Tate, poet and literary critic; and the historian of theology, Jaroslav Pelikan – to name but a few of the speakers. Although Lilly eventually cut back on its funding, the series continued at the same high level till 1981. At the time of the Program's fiftieth anniversary in 2006, support from an alumna made possible the revival of an annual "Christian Culture Lecture."

The Program has consistently attracted able students, numbering on average perhaps fifteen new majors a year – which means that in its more than half-century of existence, as many as 800 young women have graduated from Saint Mary's with degrees in Christian Culture or (after a name change in 1968) "Humanistic Studies." Since that academic background might seem unrelated to prospects for gainful employment, Bruno's promotional material underlined the point that many graduates went on to rewarding careers in education, journalism, law, business, and other lines of work.

Bruno's students unquestionably developed an intense loyalty to the Program and an equally intense affection for him as teacher and friend. His personal charm goes far toward explaining this reaction, for Bruno was a genial, out-going person with a lively mind, wide-ranging curiosity, rich erudition, and definite opinions.

How these qualities were brought to bear in terms of classroom technique is known only to his students, since he never let others sit in on his lectures. The student recollections I have seen – besides treasuring his Austrian-accented "Brunoisms" (e.g., "*I'm right once more!*") – mention his Socratic posing of questions; his insistence on their "correlating" the various facets of what they were learning; and the satisfaction they derived from an approach that brought out the distinctive character of an historical epoch, as well a coherent pattern of historical change.

The overall educational effect was captured by a former student (later a psychotherapist and professional counselor) who described Bruno as "the father of my mind."

Bruno Schlesinger and Christian Culture Students, ca. 1960.

Time and Change

Responding to a question at an alumnae gathering after his retirement, Bruno identified the early years of the Program as the period he found most rewarding. A natural enough response, since those were the heady beginnings of an experiment in which he had invested so much of himself and that had gotten off to a very good start. But more fundamentally, it was the best of times because Dawson's ideas were closely attuned to the overall pattern of Catholic thought and feeling in the mid-1950s.

A decade later, that was no longer the case. The Second Vatican Council (1962-1965) changed the way the Catholic Church understood itself, its modes of worship, its moral teachings, and its relation to other religious bodies and to the modern world. American Catholics naturally differed in how they reacted to this new understanding of what it meant to be a Catholic. But differences notwithstanding, the overall impact of the Council made the Dawsonian view of things seem outmoded – or, even worse, "triumphalist."

Daniel Callahan's comments at the time of Dawson's death in 1970 are revealing. Callahan, a former editor of *Commonweal*, had served for three years as Dawson's student assistant at Harvard. In that capacity, he acknowledged having learned much from Dawson. But being a "child of the times," Callahan was much more taken by "the new theologies of secularity, conciliar renewal, 'relevance,' and free-wheeling pluralism." Dawson's death did not, in his view, mark the end of an era because "the long period of fascination with the

24

idea of a Christian culture had come to a close at least a decade [earlier]."

By 1968, Bruno had also come to the conclusion that "Christian Culture" was no longer an attractive term. The previously mentioned name-change to "Humanistic Studies," was designed to correct two widely-held misunderstandings. Some students and parents mistakenly regarded the Christian Culture Program as "a whitewash of existing Catholic tradition" that romanticized the past. Others seemed to think it was a just another course in theology. Though he counted on the new title to eliminate these erroneous perceptions, Bruno did not intend to make basic changes in his pedagogical approach.

Judging from the fact that "HUST" (as "Humanistic Studies" soon came to be known) continued to attract its full quota of new majors, the name-change served its intended purpose. During the first decade under the new banner, Bruno continued to be the only full-time faculty member in what had long been, for all practical purposes, a free-standing academic department. It took on greater institutional elaboration over the next ten years as three new faculty positions were created. In 1978, the hiring of Gail Mandell added to the diversity of its offerings by virtue of her expertise in English, her background in Asian studies, and her sensitivity to developments in women's studies. In the 1980s, John Shinners, whose field of concentration was medieval Christianity, and Philip Hicks, a specialist in early modern Europe, also joined the HUST faculty.

By this time, Bruno had become an iconic figure at Saint Mary's. The program he founded was regarded as the jewel in Saint Mary's curricular crown, and he was often featured in Saint Mary's alumnae magazine. In 1985 he received the signal honor of being named to the "Bruno P. Schlesinger Chair in Humanistic Studies" – the first endowed chair ever established at Saint Mary's. Not the least of its perks was a reserved parking place that greatly reduced the distance the eponymous chairholder had to wade through the drifts of northern Indiana's snowy winters.

Bruno, then in his mid-seventies, had already begun to cut back on his time in the classroom. Eventually his teaching load was reduced to one course, "Art and Culture," which he continued to offer until his retirement in 2005. The luster of that occasion – and of the following year's celebration of the Christian Culture Program's fiftieth anniversary – was unhappily diminished by differences regarding curricular matters that developed between Bruno and his erstwhile colleagues in Humanistic Studies.

I do not have first-hand knowledge of the issues involved in the misunderstanding because we had moved from South Bend several years before it arose. After that, I saw Bruno only on occasional visits to Notre Dame, and he did not like to dwell on a subject painful to all concerned. Nor would it serve any useful purpose to enlarge on this rare discordant note as Saint Mary's *"Age of Schlesinger"* came to a close. Indeed, doing so would convey a distorted picture of Bruno's characteristically generous and cheerful relations with colleagues and friends.

In the years left to him, Bruno remained intellectually alert, though his health was precarious and his vision seriously impaired. He was reluctant to leave South Bend, but in June of 2010 he and Alice moved to southern California, where three of their now-adult children lived. Not long thereafter, Bruno suffered a fall and a serious fracture. And it was in Santa Barbara – the city in which he and Alice honeymooned seventy years earlier – that Bruno died on September 2, 2010.

At a memorial service held later at Saint Mary's, Gail Mandell eulogized the man with whom she had worked closely for more than a quarter century. Referring to Sir Thomas More, she likened Bruno's "sparkling wit, deep wisdom, and extraordinary learning" to that of the great humanist saint. He was, she added, a man of great "emotional complexity... [who could be] genial, stern, sweet, stubborn, shy, sly, tough, vulnerable." And as with Thomas More – whom Bruno had designated the patron saint of Humanistic Studies – it was religious faith that "supported his life's journey and inspired his life's work."

To that I would add only that his memory is treasured by the generations of grateful students to whom he was so devoted. To them, and to all the friends whose lives he enriched, Bruno Schlesinger was, indeed, "a man for all seasons."

He is rightly numbered among those of whom the psalmist wrote, "the righteous shall be in everlasting remembrance."

A NOTE ON THE SOURCES

Information about, and documents pertaining to, Bruno's early life, escape from Austria, and experience in the United States were provided by Mary Schlesinger of Santa Barbara, CA, and her siblings, Cathy, John, and Tom. The family also preserved his academic records as a graduate student at Notre Dame. His doctoral dissertation – *Christopher Dawson and the Modern Political Crisis* – was published by Notre Dame in 1949. Margaret Fosmoe's article on Bruno's retirement, which appeared in the *South Bend Tribune,* May 4, 2005, provides a brief but informative sketch of his career.

John Kovach, archivist at Saint Mary's College, was very helpful in identifying photographs and other materials relating to Bruno's teaching career. Most of the family papers are now, or soon will be, deposited in the archives of Saint Mary's College. Alan Delozier, archivist at Seton Hall University, provided copies of over a dozen letters exchanged between Bruno and Msgr. Osterreicher between 1957 and 1976. My friend and neighbor, Ruth Eckhouse, assisted me in deciphering the handwriting of Bruno's three-page memoir, which was written in German.

Gail Mandell, John Shinners, and Philip Hicks, former colleagues of Bruno in the Humanistic Studies program, responded generously to my inquiries and provided much valuable information on Bruno's career and personality. Former Christian Culture/Humanistic Studies students Paula Lawton Bevington, Mary Griffin Burns, and Mardi Hack (whose comments were relayed by my friend, Anne Kearney, a Saint Mary's graduate who majored in history) shared their recollections of Bruno. So also did Father Marvin R. O'Connell, professor emeritus of history at Notre Dame, Bruno's friend for many years.

Bruno and Humanistic Studies were featured in the following issues of the *Courier,* Saint Mary's alumnae magazine: February 1976; Spring 1982; Winter 1985; "Sesquicentennial Issue" 1994; Spring 2000; and Winter 2010. Daniel Callahan's remarks at the time of Dawson's death appeared first in *Commonweal* June 6, 1970, and were re-printed in the April 5, 1996 issue of the same magazine.

Among published works, my own *Contending with Modernity* (Oxford, 1996) elucidates the context of Catholic higher education at the time Dawson's ideas were being discussed. Gail Mandell's *Madeleva: A Biography* (State University of New York, 1997) is excellent on the situation at Saint Mary's. John Connelly's *From Enemy to Brother* (Harvard, 2011) has rich information on Father Oesterreicher's activities in Vienna in the 1930s. Adam Schwartz, "Confronting the 'Totalitarian AntiChrist': Christopher Dawson and Totalitarianism," *Catholic Historical Review* 89 (July 2003), offers a more sympathetic interpretation of Dawson's views on the topic than that set forth in Bruno's dissertation. For Dawson's life and thought more generally, see Christina Scott, *A Historian and His World* (London, 1984).

Gallery

Schlesinger Family
(from L.) Bruno, Aurelia (mother), Kurt, & Max (father) (ca. 1919-20)

Bruno (front) & Kurt Schlesinger (ca. 1917-18)

in front of the family motorcycle repair shop in Austria.

Alice & Bruno

Alice & Bruno

Alice & Bruno (possibly California)

friend, Brenton McCormick, Alice & Bruno Schlesinger
(possibly California)
Mr. McCormick acted as the witness to their wedding.

Alice & Bruno, Wedding Day, May 1940

Robert Speaight,, Patricia McGinn & Bruno Schlesinger

St. Mary's College, 1960

Class of Christian Culture Program at St. Mary's College
(ca. 1959-60)

Class of Humanistic Studies Program (HUST)

(ca. 1977-78)

Bruno with son, John

St. Mary's College President William Hickey & Bruno Schlesinger
on the occasion of Bruno receiving an honorary degree. 1994

Professor Bruno P. Schlesinger

Bruno P. Schlesinger, 1911 - 2010

Speaker List 1957-2012

Christian Culture Program / Humanisitic Studies

1957

- Yves R. Simon: Truth and Illusion in the Interpretation of Science
- George B. Flahiff: Art and Theology

1958

- Frank Sheed: History and Christopher Dawson
- Charles DeKoninck: Marxism and Human Redemption
- Robert Speaight: Paul Claudel's *Satin Slipper*
- Ewart Lewis: The Medieval Contribution to the Western Political Tradition
- Francis Fergusson: On Reading Dante in 1958
- J. M. Cameron: The Enigma of Totalitarianism
- Karl Stern: Spiritual Aspects of Psychotherapy
- Allen Tate: How Not to Read Poetry

1959

- Vernon J. Bourke : The *City of God* and the Christian View of History
- Thomas N. Brown: Catholicism and Irish Immigrant Nationalism, 1820-1860
- Christopher Dawson: Christian Culture and American Education
- Mircea Eliade: History and the Cyclical View of Time
- David M. Stanley: The Emergence of Christianity from Judaism
- Brian Tierney: Law, Justice, and Christian Society: The Contribution of the Medieval Canonists
- Myron P. Gilmore: Erasmus: The Cause of Christian Humanism in the Last Years, 1529-1536
- Louise Bogan: American Poetry at Mid-Century
- Andre Girard: Church Architecture and Modern Art

1960

- Lewis Hanke: Christian Conscience in the Spanish Conquest of America: The Contribution of Bartolomé de las Casas
- Joseph M. Kitagawa: East and West: A Dialogue
- Louis L. Martz: Henry Vaughan and the Augustinian Meditation
- Philip Scharper: The American Experiment and the Catholic Experience
- John M. Oesterreicher: The Biblical Concept of Justice
- Robert Speaight: T. S. Eliot's *The Waste Land*
- Randall Stewart: Doctrines of Man in American Literature
- Hugh Taylor: Science and Religion: Towards Unity

1961

- Yi-Pao Mei: Confucianism and Chinese Culture
- Agnes Mongan: Representations of Saint Francis and His Symbols in Art
- Jarosław Pelikan: Athens and Jerusalem: A Tale of Two Cities
- G. De Bertier: Religion in France during the Restoration
- Giles Constable: The Ordering of Society in the Middle Ages
- Ernest L. Fortin: The Church Fathers and the Transmission of the Christian Message
- Thomas Gilby: Morals in Politics

1962

- William G. Pollard: Science and Christianity in Western Civilization
- Joseph M. Kitagawa: Buddhism in the Modern World
- Charles W. Lightbody: Joan of Arc and the Historians
- Gaines Post: 'Reason of State' in the Middle Ages
- Norman St. John-Stevas: Law and Morals
- George H. Tavard: The Scope of Christian Culture

1963

- Andre Girard: The Life of Jesus
- Philip W. Powell: The Significance of Hispanophobia in the Christian West
- J. Ambrose Raftis: Christopher Dawson: Pioneer Historian of Unity
- Carl B. Cone: Burke and the Crisis of the European Order
- Alice von Hildebrand: Solitude and Communion

1964

- Adrian van Kaam: Religion and Existential Psychology
- Hajo Holborn: Leopold Ranke's Conception of History
- Paul J. Hallinan: Christian and Secular Humanism
- John C. Greene: Darwinism Yesterday and Today
- Lucetta Mowry: The Dead Sea Scrolls and the Early Church

1965

- Perry LeFevre: Kierkegaard and Christ
- Manning Pattillo: The Future of the Church College
- Franklin H. Littell: Protestant Self-Consciousness in America
- John Freccero: Dante's Vision of the Incarnation: *Paradiso* XXXIII, 131

1966

- Bernard Cooke: Christianity and Culture
- Langdon Gilkey: The 'God is Dead' Theology
- Paul Sigmund: The Catholic Church in the Developing Countries

1967

- George Lindbeck: A Protestant Reassessment of the Reformation
- George Mosse: The Appeal of Nazi Culture
- William Alfred: Tragic Concentration in *Waiting for Godot*
- Alden Fisher: Contemporary Psychoanalysis and Religious Values

1968

- Martin Marty: American Consensus, American Conflict: Past and Future
- Richard Sylvester: Vision and Re-Vision in Thomas More's *Utopia*
- Robert Gleason: The Christian Meaning of Death
- Charles Long: God and Silence: The Significations of Modernity

1969

- Josef Altholz: The Conscience of Lord Acton
- Seymour Halleck: Student Values in a Changing World
- Dexter Hanley: The Conscientious Objector: Evolution or Revolution

1970

- Erich Heller: Bertolt Brecht
- Robert Byrnes: The Dreyfus Affair: The Twentieth Century Begins
- Henry Margenau: The Role of Science in Human Experience
- Erich Heller: Nietzsche

1971

- Jarosław Pelikan: Luther Comes to the New World
- Erich Heller: Literature and Social Responsibility
- Joseph Schwab: Liberal Arts for Now

1972

- Erich Heller: Franz Kafka
- Hanna Gray: Machiavelli and the Humanist Tradition

1973

- Erich Heller: Shame and Shamelessness in the Age of Pornography
- Vera Dunham: Alexander Solzhenitzyn
- James Billington: The Strange Death of Liberal Education Victor Turner: Pilgrimages From Within

1974

- Robert Speaight: Francois Mauriac: The Tension Between God and Mammon in His Life and Work
- Stanley Idzerda: Reflections on Our Permanent Revolution

1975

- James Hennesey: The American Catholic Experience
- Karl Weintraub: Benjamin Franklin and the Protestant Ethic
- Erich Heller: Autobiography and Literature: *Death in Venice*
- Karl Weintraub: Abelard: A Question about Individuality

1976

- Nancy McCormick Rambusch: Montessori Education for American Children
- Thomas Brown: The Immigrant and the Bicentennial: The Boston Experience

1977

- Jarosław Pelikan: The Spirit of Medieval Theology
- Helene Roberts: Images of Women in Art and Literature: Mother Earth and the Warrior Maiden
- Marilyn Stokstad: Women Artists in the Renaissance
- Erich Heller: Psychology and Modern Literature

1978

- John A. Garraty: Work and Idleness in Modern Societies
- Janel Mueller: The Drama and Enigma of the Self: Donne's Art of the Lyric
- Joseph Kennedy: The Role of Women in Northeast India
- Erich Heller: Literature and Social Responsibility

1979

- Jarosław Pelikan: The Gospel According to Lev Tolstoy
- James Redfield: Socratic Education

1980

- Lawrence Stone: Love and Marriage in Eighteenth-Century England
- Thomas Lawler: Thomas More and the Art of Dying Well
- Erich Heller: Dr. Faustus – Is He Damned or Saved?
- Monica Schuler: African Culture in the New World

1981

- Elizabeth Helsinger: Victim or Villain? The Passionate Heroines of Pre-Raphaelite Art

2006

- Miri Rubin: "Mary: From Jewish Maiden to Global Icon"

2007

- Patricia Hampl: "Sacrament of Self: The Catholic Roots of Contemporary Memoir"

2008

- María Rosa Menocal: "Poetry as an Act of History: Al-Andalus, Sefarad, Spain"

2009

- William Chester Jordan: "Crusader Prologues: Preparations for War in the Gothic Age"

2010

- Thomas Cahill: "The End of Christain Divisions: Achieving Reunion through Truth-Telling"

2011

- Mary Gordon: "The Uses and Limits of Outrage: A Meditation on the work of Francisco Goya, Czeslaw Milosz and Denise Levertov"

2012

- James Carroll: "The Reforming Dimension of Christianity in Western Culture: Vatican II and Beyond"

Bruno P. Schlesinger, 1911 - 2010

Bruno Schlesinger: The Father of My Mind

Patricia Ferris McGinn,[2] Class of 1960

Reprinted from Courier, Vol. 56 #1, Spring 1982

Dr. Schlesinger never quite fit behind the classroom desk. Whenever he tried to cross his legs, there would be a great banging and thumping as he and the desk battled it out.

To his students, his influence cannot really be contained either. It has a way of thumping into our approach to many experiences and tasks. It bangs against all the tendencies in our culture to compartmentalize, specialize, individualize experience and knowledge.

Last summer I met a recent Humanistic Studies graduate who worked in the education department of the New York Metropolitan Museum of Art. She told me of her struggle to change their approach toward presenting art within its cultural context. Here she was, at 22 years old, telling the Met how to present art – to present it the way Bruno Schlesinger would have. I understood her perfectly.

Not long afterward, I was reflecting on my own career as a counselor and therapist, and I realized how much Bruno has influenced me, too. I approach a person or a family in the same way Bruno taught me to approach Western civilization – tracing the "red thread" of a theme or a pattern, trying to make sense of a life in terms of an individual interacting with his family history, with contemporary culture, and with personally significant events. Bruno taught me how to make connections, to see how one set of values and patterns interact with another, how present realities make sense in terms of past ones, and how the past, transformed, is alive in the present. This way of thinking is his legacy to me and, I believe, to all of his students. That is why I call him the "Father of my mind."

Teaching us this way of thinking, however, was not easy. I remember the first few weeks of class how tough and intimidating

---

2 Patricia Ferris McGinn is a psychotherapist, licensed professional counselor and former executive director of the Illinois Mental Health Counselors Association. She teaches in the art therapy program at the School of the Art Institute of Chicago. She is a co-author with Bernard McGinn of *Early Christian Mystics, The Divine Vision of the Spiritual Masters* (Crossroads, 2003)

Bruno was. He challenged us constantly, pushing, pulling, shaming us into comprehending the material and articulating it accurately. He invited us daily to change our majors, to consider that perhaps this was not our "cup of tea," to get into another program while there was still time. Yet most of us hung on, fought off our insecurities, complained and resisted, but learned to conform to "his way."

Then we had our first test. Our prose flowed across the page as we, by now verbally proficient, waxed eloquent about the early Christian martyrs. We soon found that the writing skill that had earned many an "A" before would not pull us through. Bruno cut us to ribbons. Beautiful descriptions would not do; the facts had to be accurate and the themes clearly organized. There was simply no way around him; "sloppy thinking" got the same treatment as the underside of his desk. Bruno and the desk never did make peace, but we were more malleable. Slowly our sloppy thinking started to shape up, his way.

Bruno was tough, but he was also vulnerable. His tender side showed through in his love for his children and his profound sense of family and parenthood. We soon realized that we, too, were somehow family to him. Although Bruno did not entertain us at his home, and we rarely sought him as a counselor, a familial sense of identity and cohesiveness developed among us. He was concerned for us and was intent on forming our interior and intellectual lives in deep and lasting ways. As we learned in later years, he continued to follow our personal and professional lives with paternal interest. Like a father, he wanted us to find success and happiness for ourselves, but he also hoped we would be a credit to him and to the formation he had given us.

Today, he has a bulletin board outside his office in Madeleva Hall. It is covered with postcards from students who have finally seen the Sistine Chapel or Hagia Sophia, and had to let him know. There are announcements of higher degrees, of weddings and new jobs, and there are baby pictures. His students know that their accomplishments matter to him, and they want to share their families and their successes with him. It is very moving to one who graduated over 20 years ago to see that someone who graduated two years ago has the same sense of attachment and loyalty both from him and to him. I have heard other teachers refer to "Bruno and his girls" with a funny shake of the head; the attachment seem special to them, too.

When I mentally put myself back in a rumpled pink golfer and runny nylons, I discover memories of Bruno that are less profound but equally precious. He was, and is, a European gentleman, who hastens to take care to walk on the correct side of a lady. As a student, I always got confused, thinking he had ducked into a doorway or fallen down a manhole when he zipped behind me to get on the "right" side as we walked.

Bruno's Viennese heritage was apparent in his custom of afternoon coffee and cookies, but most of all in his commitment to the arts and his gallant effort to impart love of high culture to the likes of me. Whenever his pet committee, the Concert and Lecture Series, sponsored an event, he not only encouraged us to go, but also expected us to comment in class the next day about the experience. To this day I wonder to what extent the money I spend on tickets, parking and babysitting to maintain season tickets to the opera and symphony is due to the time Bruno looked at me in class, shook his head in sad disbelief and said, "You are just not a music voman."

A rich personality has many sides, and Bruno is no exception. He can be humorous, gloomy, critical, optimistic and cranky, but there are other, much deeper, sides which he keeps hidden. I have never heard him talk about his early life, for instance, or the suffering he endured in leaving his homeland. I believe that he is deeply religious and a truly passionate man, but he does not disclose much about such private realms.

A sketch of Bruno necessarily includes his wife, Alice, whose own profession as an artist has recently been brought to the College in a splendid portrait of Sister Madeleva. Alice has nurtured their children, established her own place in the community, and supported Bruno's work. Their life together has been largely a private matter, yet Alice has always been a presence in my consciousness of Bruno and his life.

In 1956, Bruno's Christian Culture was an innovative program. Today, as Humanistic Studies, it is still unusual, when even fewer people recognize the name of Christopher Dawson. But the Saint Mary's in which Bruno's program took shape had a clear understanding and a unified commitment to traditional liberal arts education. It was a Saint Mary's which, for better or for worse, exposed every freshman to the *Trivium* and to two years of liberal arts curriculum before they began in their majors.

By today's standards it was a curriculum in some respects incredibly narrow, but at the same time it was immensely rich in its integrative approach to knowledge and its strong appreciation for learning as such. Bruno's program did not then and does not now exist in a vacuum; Bruno has always made it clear that he counts on his students' exposure to theology, philosophy, literature and languages in other courses.

In fact, many of us were influenced by such powerful teachers as Sister Miriam Joseph, Sister Franzita and Sister Maria Pieta, not to mention the stubborn little poet who enabled and enriched the whole enterprise from the president's office.

For those who love learning and the liberal arts, this interdisciplinary program and the richly educated man who embodies it have irresistible appeal.

Bruno's Song

Mary Griffin Burns[3]

Notes by Philip Gleason

This song was sung to Bruno by the class at an end-of-semester party just before they graduated in 1962.

This very witty song gives some sense of the scope of the program, and brings out the degree to which Bruno insisted on students bringing together what they were learning from different kinds of sources (art, literature, theology, history, etc.) in what he called "correlation."

Sung to the tune of "The Vicar of Bray" -- a satiric ditty about a clergymen whose parish (or "living") was a place called "Bray," which was in Ireland in the days it was under British rule.

He (the Vicar) promises that "whatsoever king may reign" (Catholic, Protestant, High Church Anglican, Low Church Anglican...) he'll adjust his belief accordingly, and "*still be the Vicar of Bray, sir!*"

---

3 Mary Griffin Burns graduated with the 1962 class at St. Mary's College. After college she went to law school at Northwestern University. She is the Supervisory Attorney, Office of the Public Guardian, Chicago.

Bruno's Song, written by Mary Griffin Burns
From the Class of 1962 to Bruno

When Trajan ruled the world of Rome,
And Christians were tabu, sir.
Young Pliny wrote a letter home,
And asked him what to do, sir!

And this is how we will maintain,
Until our graduation,
That whether or not the facts are plain,
They'll still need correlation!

King Charlemagne was fond of books,
But only read in bed, sir.
He fought for unity of mind,
By chopping Saxon heads, sir!

When monks were bold in simony
And courtly love hurrayed, sir,
The loyal knights of Christendom,
Were saved in a crusade, sir!

Sweet Abelard was logical,
Fuzzy thinking he bemoaned, sir.
But after he met Heloise,
He mixed up *"sic et non"*, sir!

The schism made it hard to tell,
The real pope from the rest, sir.
If all the saints weren't even sure,
Have mercy on our test, sir!

Pascal didn't like the Jesuits.
He thought them quite a hoax, sir.
Such minor squabbles helped enrich
The age we call Baroque, sir!

When Kierkegaard said "either/or"
Regina lost her man, sir.
We want to be real Christian too,
But that's a big demand, sir!

To show us that there's more to life,
Than we had ever guessed, sir.
You asked Confucius what he says..
He says "The West is Best," sir!

The French Revolution held the key
To the 19th Century cults, sir.
It led in: liberalism, nationalism, democracy
        As well as socialism, pragmatism,
        Modernism, positivism, Romanticism
        And social Darwinism

And locked in Christian Culture!

To keep our mental *habitus*,
We'll still read Maritain, sir.
But we'll keep both our man and books,
Dr. Christian says you can, sir!

In Christian Culture, we have seen,
There'll always be a key, sir.
In simple English, this does mean,
Thou art our cup of tea, sir!

A Talk with Professor Bruno Schlesinger

Nancy Fallon[4]

Courier, *Spring 2000*

We met in his office in Madeleva, an office where books crown the shelves and papers clutter the working surface of the desk. Arthritis may have slowed Bruno Schlesinger, but nothing has slowed the pace of his mind or dampened his passion for learning, his interest in people, or his dry wit. As I set out the tape recorder for our interview, he couldn't resist bemoaning that his strong Central European accent couldn't be transmitted in print: "I tell students that it is the same accent as Arnold Schwarzenegger, but it doesn't seem to impress them."

Schlesinger, who came to this country from his native Austria to finish a doctorate in history and political science at Notre Dame, first taught at Saint Mary's while a graduate student, lecturing on the history of art and Western civilization. In 1945 he joined the faculty as an assistant professor. During his 40 years of full-time teaching, Schlesinger conceived, lobbied for, and developed the Christian Culture Program (later renamed Humanistic Studies). Alternately intimidating and enthralling students with his wide-ranging knowledge and his exacting standards, he succeeded in drawing talented student and cementing the program's place in the College's humanities curriculum.

He became the first recipient of the Spes Unica Excellence in Teaching Award and the first holder of an endowed chair at Saint Mary's, the Bruno Schlesinger Chair of Humanistic Studies.

Schlesinger resists the suggestion that he had a significant impact on campus culture ("I was just very, very isolated in our little bailiwick.") or that he was a demanding teacher ("I never felt tough.... But I did have to insist on certain standards."). Instead he

---

4 Nancy Fallon was editor of the Saint Mary's alumnae magazine Courier for three years from 1997 to 2000. She died unexpectedly in February of 2000 at age 45. Fallon began as a freelance writer for Courier in 1989. She also worked as a freelance writer for Notre Dame Magazine.

In 1981, she married Stephen Fallon, the Rev. John J. Cavanaugh, Professor of the Humanities at Notre Dame.

is happier talking at length about the ideas of Christopher Dawson, the scholar whose theories of western civilization formed the foundation for the Christian Culture Program, the challenges of college teaching and, of course, the generations of students he taught at St. Mary's.

You have been an important part of Saint Mary's for many years. What changes have you observed in the climate of the campus during that time?

When I joined the faculty of Stint Mary's in 1945, most of the administrative and faculty positions were held by Sisters of the Holy Cross. While this setup would strike some people as a throwback to days gone by, others would interpret it as an early expression of the women's movement.

The "Sister/Professors" managed to combine their religious vocations with the demands of the academic profession. They did it with grace and competency, often in a spirit of warmhearted generosity. Alumnae returning to the campus reminisce about some of these extraordinary women: Sister Maria Pieta, Sister Benedictus, Sister Marie Rosaire and many others.

Quite a few of our best students, drawn to a religious vocation and to this lifestyle, entered the community of the Holy Cross Sisters and subsequently became members of the faculty.

As the numbers of Sisters began to diminish over time, an even larger number of laymen and laywomen appeared on the scene. No doubt they made major contributions, but the spiritual atmosphere which the community had created could not be duplicated.

One of the things that alumnae often tell me is that they learned self-discipline at Saint Mary's. Are tomorrow's graduates learning the same thing?

On the whole, students graduating from Saint Mary's 40 or 50 years ago were extremely disciplined and focused on learning. Social life was narrowly circumscribed: a rare movie, the weekly tea dance, no alcohol, an occasional trip downtown. As an alumna told me, "There was nothing else to do but study!" It was an austere regime, but it had its rewards, such as experiencing the joys of intellectual life.

Things are different now. The contemporary student, haunted by a myriad of distractions, tends to fritter away precious hours and days. Fortunately there are many exceptions, but the waste of time can be easily linked to a decline of academic standards.

That begs the question: Were you as tough a teacher as many say you were?

I believe that every class develops its own scholastic standards. What I tried to do was to persuade students to maintain their own self-set standards on a regular basis. That is not toughness.

Tell me about the formation of the Christian Culture Program, now called Humanistic Studies, which you developed in the 1950s.

The 1940s and 1950s were marked by lively discussions about the undergraduate curriculum. Critics complained that excessive specialization had led to a loss of unity and to meaningless fragmentation.

In 1953, the distinguished English scholar, Christopher Dawson, offered his ideas on education. He recommended that the achievements of Christian culture in history, literature, art and social and spiritual thought be studies as interrelated factors.

The purpose of Dawson's recommendation was two-fold: to restore a semblance of unit to the undergraduate curriculum, and to initiate the student into a great living tradition, providing her with a perspective for contemporary issues.

Dawson's highly original ideas cause considerable discussion. Although a number of outstanding scholars and writers supported it, the Catholic establishment, mainly administrators, rejected it.

I was most enthusiastic about Dawson's program and sent a memo to Sister Madeleva pleading for the adoption of a Christian Culture Program as an interdisciplinary major. As it turned out, Dawson's ideas were in harmony with Sister Madeleva's thoughts.

A long time passed before Sister Madeleva decided to adopt the program, but I was finally appointed as chairman and the journey began in 1956 with me functioning as the sole faculty member. Later renamed the Humanistic Studies Program, it remains a viable major.

How has the program evolved over the years?

With the arrival of Gail Mandell, the program was greatly enhanced – both in terms of curriculum and personality. Her offering in Asian literature brought a new dimension to our course. She generated a quality of trust and confidence. The program expanded further with the addition of two fine scholars: John Shinners and Philip Hicks.

Our students reacted favorably to the interdisciplinary approach. They appreciated the discovery of a a rich tradition. To read and discuss Dante or Thomas More or Pascal appeared to be more rewarding than a dry textbook.

But parents didn't always share the same appreciation of the program as their daughters.

That's true. Some parents were afraid that an "impractical" major would deprive their daughters of a livelihood. The reality was that our students proved to be extraordinarily marketable. They now work in many fields: as university and college teachers, lawyers, physicians, governmental employees, bankers, stockbrokers, social workers, managers, etc. one of our majors became a nun, while another is a CEO. Some women choose marriage and motherhood as their profession.

What bound you to Saint Mary's all those years?

There were many reasons for staying at Saint Mary's, including a pleasant work environment and congenial, helpful colleagues. There were no "backstairs intrigues" at Saint Mary's.
A more persuasive and compelling factor was the opportunity to develop Dawson's program, brilliant though badly misunderstood. At Saint Mary's, I enjoyed an atmosphere of absolute independence. Nobody ever interfered with my work. Best of all, there were the wonderful students: enthusiastic, cooperative, good-humored and intelligent. They translated a paper model into living reality.

And your ties to Saint Mary's continue?

I teach one course a year, usually "Art and Culture," a history of Western paintings beginning with the Renaissance. I find this very enjoyable. It keeps one in touch with colleagues, students and, in a way, with the life of the College.

Bruno P. Schlesinger, 1911 - 2010

Reflections on Bruno Schlesinger

Gail Porter Mandell[5]

September 22, 2010

> *"He was a man of angel's wit and singular learning;*
> *I know not his fellow.*
> *For where is the man of that gentleness, lowliness, and affability?*
> *And as time requireth, a man of marvellous mirth and pastimes;*
> *and sometimes of as sad gravity:*
> *a man for all seasons."*

Those words were famously written of Thomas More, the 16th century saint and humanist, whom Bruno Schlesinger chose as the patron saint of the Christian Culture/Humanistic Studies Program. They describe Bruno himself equally well.

Like his hero More, Bruno was indeed a man of sparkling wit, deep wisdom, and extraordinary learning. He, too, delighted in good company – usually over lunch or tea in Bruno's case. Also like More, Bruno was a man of great emotional complexity. He could be genial, stern, sweet, stubborn, shy, sly, tough, vulnerable. He was a man whose religious faith supported his life's journey and inspired his life's work.

Born a Jew, Bruno's faith sprang from the faith of Moses, Abraham, Isaac and Jacob, and his faith both before and after his conversion to Christianity was, as the passage from the Gospel of Luke so joyfully puts it, a faith in "a God of the living" – a God whose spirit, as Paul writes, renews us daily.

I was privileged to know Bruno for almost 40 years and to work side by side with him for over 30 of them. That's quite a few seasons, and every season I spent with Bruno brought revelations and surprises. He was already over sixty when we met, which for most of us begins the winter of life, but Bruno was born in the spring, and his spirit was eternally spring-like.

There was a child-like playfulness about him, and it came out most obviously around children, in whom he took special delight. Some of us will remember the big bulletin board outside his office, which was papered not with wise quotations or reproductions of famous works of art but with snapshots of alums and their children and, eventually, their

---

5 Gail Porter Mandell is Emerita Professor at St. Mary's College and Emerita of Bruno P. Schlesinger Chair in Humanistic Studies, and author of *Madeleva: One Woman's Life* (Paulist Press, 1995); and *Madeleva: A Biography* (SUNY Press, 1997).

grandchildren. When alums brought their kids back to visit, as they often do, Bruno dropped everything and brought out his toys and stash of goodies: his "Perpetual Motion Bird" (not even Einstein could figure out how that thing worked, he always pointed out), his giant-sized M&M dispenser, and his Pepperidge Farm cookies (he loved those Milanos).

I could easily imagine Bruno as a boy sneaking a ride on one of the bikes in his parents' bicycle, motorcycle and repair shop in the town near Vienna where he was born. He left his native Austria in 1938, six months after Nazi occupation. He was in his twenties then, close to finishing a law degree.

As old age set in, he took his first and, so far as I am aware, his only trip to his motherland. When he returned, he told me that it was as if all the intervening years – his life in America, even his marriage and children – had all been a dream. It was, he said, as though he'd never left Vienna, and it was hard to leave a second time. What he missed the most, he told me, was life in the city, especially sitting in one of the Viennese coffee shops for hours on end, ordering a strudel with his coffee and talking with friends about life.

Not that he didn't love life here. He had his teaching career, which as he said with characteristic understatement, had worked out "pretty well" for him. He had his "Liesl" - the name which I always heard him address Alice at home – the four children and, late in life, his four grandchildren. As Alice told me early on, "He doesn't like to talk about himself." But every now and then, he'd share a story about John, Mary, Kathy or Tom, or about Tom and Kathy's children, and you realized how enormously proud he was of those too close to his heart for easy words.

Not true of politics, however, which was his favorite topic, with music and art as close seconds. Those he eagerly talked about. Art and music engaged his intellect through emotions, but politics aroused his passions – and the more local the politics, the more passionate he could become. He didn't bother about minor brouhahas, but a serious controversy could occasion multiple daily drop-ins ("Last time, I promise," he'd say after his third or fourth visit. Two minutes later, Bruno in the doorway: "Just one more thing---.") There were nightly phone calls too, if there was a really hot one. At such times his mind was like a threshing machine: sharp, cutting, sifting and sorting.

Nothing in my day, however could match the intense negotiation required to create the Christian Culture Program. It threatened the status quo, and so, he said, his proposal "almost died before it could be born." In spite of many delays and obstacles, his political acuity combined with his passionate persistence brought the Program of Christian Culture, eventually renamed "Humanistic Studies," into being.

And what a triumph it was! Unique in its focus on the study of Christian culture as a way to interpret the modern world, the Program soon became one of the hallmarks of a Saint Mary's education – the *"department deluxe,"* as Sister Madeleva called it. Its interdisciplinary curriculum and emphasis on liberal learning have sustained it through more than half a century. The lives and achievements of its alums are the best evidence of the Program's enduring strength and relevance.

A large part of the success of the Program was, beyond a doubt, was Bruno himself and his great gifts as a teacher. His Socratic method, requiring mental discipline and close attention from students, his keen sense of what he called the "unifying threads" of culture as well as the "big picture" of history, his flair for drama, his masterly storytelling, his Puck-ish sense of humor – all that, plus his great personal charm, ensured that students did not forget him nor what he taught them. Walking through a museum or reading the morning paper, it all comes back, grads tell me. He initiated students into the excitement and wonder of the intellectual life, in a Christian context that engaged their mind and enlarged their faith.

His students' praise and affection turned Bruno into the legend he became. As Patricia McGinn put it so well, he became the "father of my mind." His response? "At least I never mothered them!" The devotion he inspired in his students resulted not only from their appreciation and gratitude for the education they received but also from the strong personal connection he forged with so many of them. He spent hours conversing with students in his office. His great secret was that he was a superb listener. He was interested in what interested others. It was as though he had a mental file on each of us that reminded him of all we cared about most.

Watching Bruno, I learned most of what I know about teaching and learning, although his actual advice was scant. Most of what he said came in asides, often in the form of aphorisms, a bit like the cryptic koans a zen master assigns his disciple for meditation.

For example, "It's good THEY do the work."

And: "Remind them what they know."

Or the most severe: "They come asking for bread. God forbid we give them stones."

Sharing the same birthday, Bruno and I would usually have lunch each April 15th to celebrate. When I turned fifty, he said something to console me that I've often repeated to others: "Fifty is the prime of life, Professor Mandell. You have the benefit of experience and, if you are lucky, your body isn't breaking down yet."

As Paul reminds us in his second letter to the Corinthians, even though the outer person inevitably falls into decay, the risen Christ renews the spirit of the inner person day by day. Paul, the tent maker, aptly assures us that as Christians we trust that "when the tent that we live in on earth is folded up, there is a house built by God for us, an everlasting home not made by human hands."

I believe that as we pray together today for Bruno, who has reached his everlasting home, and for his family and all who miss his earthly presence, Bruno is also praying for us, most likely the prayer of Thomas More himself: "Pray for me as I shall pray for thee, that we may merrily meet in heaven."

Bruno Schlesinger Among Friends

Marvin R. O'Connell[6]

I was the last of the Mohicans, the last, that is, of the friends Bruno Schlesinger made among the faculty at Notre Dame. The least too, because I was the youngest, nearly twenty years younger than Bruno himself. No special virtue in me; simply put, the others died or moved away from northern Indiana and I remained, so that at the end, just before his departure for California, I was his final academic dinner or luncheon companion. That assertion sounds a bit pompous, but it is really not inaccurate. By it I mean that if anyone overheard our conversations, he would have no difficulty concluding that we were a couple of old professors hashing over subjects which to the listener probably had little relationship to the real world

We talked about books, some contemporary, some more venerable. It will come as no surprise that the name and works of Christopher Dawson came up often. We discussed the political scene with Bruno usually adopting positions somewhat to the left of mine—no real radicalism, I assure you, but nevertheless, donning more frequently than I would have done the mantle of *The New York Times.* (As his sight grew more problematic he regularly hired students to read the newspaper-of-record to him.) Nor did we fail to address some of those abstract questions of universal relevance that savants from Plato to Wilfrid Sellars had tried to solve, without, in our opinion, notable success. More fun, however, was the exchange of gossip we might indulge in about our colleagues at St. Mary's and Notre Dame.

These occasions, you see, were all about talk, about conversation. Bruno was pretty much indifferent to food, the more so the older he got. His interest in alcohol was minimal. As for me,

---

6 Father O'Connell has been a member of the Notre Dame faculty since 1972. In addition to numerous articles and essays in scholarly and popular journals, Father O'Connell authored *The Oxford Conspirators: A History of the Oxford Movement 1833-1845* (University Press of America, 1969) and the definitive biography of Notre Dame's founder, *Edward Sorin* (University of Notre Dame Press, 2001)

the cuisine at the old Notre Dame University Club, where most of our meetings took place, was barely tolerable, but the availability of the Dewars White Label scotch soothed the taste buds satisfactorily. Still, chatter as we would about everything under the sun, one avenue of inquiry we seldom trod. Curious as I was and try as I might, I could not get Bruno to speak much about himself, about the converted Jew who had fled Vienna in the wake of the Nazi *Anschluss* of 1938 to become the icon of a Catholic women's college in the American Midwest. Oh, he would drop a hint now and then, perhaps about the interrogation by the Gestapo he endured, or about the time—mercifully brief—he spent in a French prison as an illegal immigrant; or, once arrived in the United States, about the hard times in California during the early 1940s, when he drifted from odd job to odd job, a door-to-door Fuller Brush salesman for a while and then a soda jerk. Fortunately, Bruno's friend (and mine), Professor Philip Gleason, with the inestimable help of the Schlesinger children, has deftly put together an account of those early years, as much of the story anyway as we are likely to get.

One day, early in 1942—in retrospect a providential moment—Bruno Schlesinger, having taken momentary refuge in the reading room of the LosAngeles public library, paged through a copy of *The Review of Politics,* where he saw notice of a graduate program in political science to be offered at the University of Notre Dame; included were instructions as to how to apply for acceptance. Young Mr. Schlesinger promptly sent off the required information to the university. Consider what a bold gamble this decision represented. Bruno knew nothing about the ins and outs of American higher education. English was an acquired language and hence for him an unpredictable means of expression. And for one of his background and experience, no place on earth could have seemed more alien than a small town in Indiana. But now he was thirty-one years old, and his life was slipping away in futility. So with the support of his beloved Alice—they had been married in 1940—he decided to take the risk. The upshot was that having been admitted into the program and granted some modest financial assistance, the Schlesingers by the autumn of 1942 had settled in South Bend. It took seven years of hard academic work to earn the doctorate, a slow pace dictated in part by the reasons cited above, and also by another intervention of Providence. In 1945 Bruno was offered a part-time teaching position at St. Mary's College. Sixty years later he retired.

Thus he entered, professionally, a feminine world. His students of course were women, as were overwhelmingly his faculty colleagues, many of whom wore the nineteenth century habit of the Sisters of the Holy Cross. The same order of nuns administered the college and did so with uncommon success. Notable among them was Mary Madeleva Wolff who served as president of the college from 1934 to 1961. The author of upwards of twenty books, Sister Madeleva exerted a strong influence in Catholic higher education circles, and her poetry was read and appreciated by a very wide public. Locally she enjoyed a reputation for plain speaking. When lesser powers in the college's hierarchy had dismissed them, it was to her that Professor Schlesinger—as we may now call him—brought his plans for a Christian Culture Program. As one who had seen many para-academic projects come and go, she hesitated at first. But Bruno's persistence prevailed in the end, so that when Sister Madeleva left office, she could place the Program near the top of the list of her many accomplishments.

(I did not know Bruno till years after Sister Madeleva's death in 1964. Nor did he speak of her very often in my hearing. When he did, he expressed a kind of wary respect for her, not unlike his general attitude toward authority figures. He did once tell me of his hilarious attempt to explain to her the principle of the "living wage" as it applied to laymen with families teaching in Catholic colleges.)

From 1956 the carefully structured and Dawson-inspired Christian Culture Program formed the center of Schlesinger's teaching at St. Mary's. But long before that, and long afterward too, he made a deep impression on the student body, as a host of alumnae across the country can attest to. I live now in a retirement community—contiguous, incidentally, to St. Mary's—where some of the oldest of those alumnae are residents, women whose memory of college days goes back to the 1940s and 1950s. Merely the mention of the name Bruno Schlesinger brings forth from these friends and neighbors of mine enthusiastic endorsements. "The best teacher I ever had"; "What a wonderful man"; "He opened for me so many intellectual doors"; "He so enriched my life, helped me to appreciate art and music and even to untangle the mysteries of politics and of social relationships." No doubt a measure of this praise is traceable to Bruno's immense personal charm. But it also reflected the consistently high quality of his instruction, the supple way in which he brought so many intellectual strands into a harmonious whole. Topping off the adventures in the classroom were the frequent evening lectures by distinguished scholars—many of them intellectual celebrities—which breathed new vigor into what otherwise might have seemed dull and pedestrian subjects. And Professor Schlesinger raised the needed funds to pay for the visits of these worthies to campus.

The fit for him at St. Mary's thus proved mutually happy and beneficial. But there was another constituency that quite naturally appealed to him, a masculine one of like minded academics to be found just across the road at Notre Dame. Or, in the first instance, nearer than that. The Schlesingers lived on Miner Street, a few blocks from the old St. Joseph's Hospital, next door to the Corbetts. James Corbett, product of the famed Ecole Nationale des Chartes in Paris, was a professor of history at Notre Dame. A gentle, courteous but purposeful man, qualities that shone clearly in the courses he taught in medieval history, Jim Corbett had interests that ranged beyond textual criticism of fourteenth century documents and even beyond the books he published on the papacy and world history. It is doubtful that he and Bruno exchanged Miner Street gossip across the backyard fence. But surely there came to be a meeting of minds between them when conversing about the Nazi menace; after all, Corbett had translated Yves Simon's bitter account of the moral and political collapse of the French Third Republic, under the title *The Road to Vichy, 1918-1938*.

Professor Corbett was well acquainted with German-born Anton-Hermann Chroust; the two of them had published jointly an edition of a fifteenth century political treatise. Professor Chroust was a big, loud, and silver-tongued polymath who divided his considerable talent and energy for study between the law and classical philosophy. Outside the classroom he presided over one corner of the cafeteria located on the ground floor in Notre Dame's south dining hall—the "pay caf," as it was popularly known, long since gone. Here there hummed the constant flow of conversation that may have been interrupted by pedagogical necessity once in a while but never really ceased. Joining in softly on occasion was Lewis Nicholson, professor of old English, as diffident as Chroust was exuberant. And here Bruno Schlesinger found a warm welcome. He could hear about Chroust's current project, just published as "The Meaning of Time in the Ancient World." Or, on a lighter note, about the red convertible Chroust always took with him on his summer holiday in Europe. Nicholson had no such exotic tale to tell, but his deep knowledge of the Beowulf story and indeed of the whole of Anglo Saxon culture, revealed in a series of prestigious publications, gave to his rare interventions an eloquence of their own. I must admit I never read any of the books written by these two pay-caf denizens, but in London, twenty years or so ago, I saw on display in the window of a second hand book store, *Aristotle: New Light on his Life and on some of his Lost Works*, by Anton-Hermann Chroust.

These were only two of the many academic friendships Bruno made at Notre Dame over the years. Still, it is worth stressing that they were typical. Chroust and Nicholson were men of real accomplishment, precisely the kind of person Schlesinger sought out. And precisely the kind who cultivated him, for these relationships were always matters of give and take. The same can be said about about the distinguished Hungarian diplomat, István Kertész, who had fled the Communists much as Schlesinger had fled the Nazis. Kertész, who combined the elegant demeanor of a Hapsburg-era aristocrat with warm Christian sensitivity, knew intuitively that Bruno understood, as could few others, the horrors he had endured during the siege of Budapest in 1945 and its bloody aftermath. And Bruno could understand too how Steven— as we all called him, our familiarity tempered by deep respect— found new life and vigor at a welcoming Notre Dame, testified to among other ways by the scholarly books he wrote, like *Between Russia and the West* and *Diplomacy and Values*.

But since it was *The Review of Politics* that had, so to speak, summoned Bruno Schlesinger to Notre Dame and St. Mary's, it should come as no surprise that it was within the *Review's* inner circle that he formed his closest bonds. The founder of the *Review* and its editor till he died in 1954 was Waldemar Gurian, a giant figure in the social sciences during the middle third of the twentieth century. Like Bruno, he was a Jewish convert to Catholicism who in the thirties had had to depart his native Germany. When he arrived at Notre Dame, however, he maintained the air of a Teutonic Herr Professor Doktor which he presumed to be his by right—as indeed it was. Bruno deeply admired him, but, like everybody else, was intimidated by him. Two thousand years ago Cicero observed that genuine friendship could be formed only between equals. Waldemar Gurian admitted of no equals.

Far different was the case with two of Gurian's associates in the operation of the *Review* and his successors as it editor. Mathew Anthony Fitzsimons—nicknamed "Bob" from his childhood—professor of history, was a large, seemingly placid person, immensely learned, of a sweet disposition, self-deprecating to a fault. The books he wrote on modern British history and historiography, like the courses he taught, were the fruit of relentlessly thorough research. Bob collected African tribal masks, and in music he favored Haydn's string quartets above all else. Beneath his apparent placidity there seethed a powerful drive to right wrongs, to see that justice be done in Church and in state. Born in the Bronx and educated at Columbia, during the mid-thirties he matriculated at Oxford and spent a brief time in Spain during the civil war. Out of these experiences he emerged as a man of the moderate left, and so pretty much shared Bruno's world view. It was a joy to witness them exchanging anecdotes.

(Many years ago, in London, I had the honor of dining with Bob at Simpson's in the Strand. Always aware of honorable custom, he handed a shilling to the man who carved our roast beef table-side.)

"My dear fellow, I couldn't agree with you more." This was an affirmation all his friends hoped to hear from Thomas J. Stritch, because of the fondness in which they held him and also because they recognized his native shrewdness. Of course sometimes "agree" gave way to "disagree," but seldom did such a reversal happen to Bruno Schlesinger; most of the time he and Tom Stritch were of one mind. Tom was the quintessential Notre Dame man. With the financial support of his uncle Samuel Stritch (later cardinal archbishop of Chicago), he arrived on campus from Nashville as a freshman in 1930, and, except for a four year stretch as a naval officer during World War II, he never left. For a good many years he served as one of the famous Notre Dame "bachelor dons," unmarried professors who lived in the dormitories and thus came to relate extraordinarily well with undergraduates. Curiously, he came to have an almost obsessive interest in the various trees that grew on campus, all of whose lineage he managed to codify. He once told me that the only woman he ever considered proposing to was his dear friend, Flannery O'Connor. Short, stocky, with a rich bass voice that sounded like apples rolling round the bottom of a barrel, Tom Stritch, every inch the alpha male, was a much lauded professor of journalism and, later, of American studies. For Bruno, whether in a light or in a shadowed mood, Tom remained always a bright light. On a discussion over some issue the essence of which I have long since forgotten, I can still recall how Bruno's face lit up when Tom said to him in his booming voice, "My dear fellow, you've got it exactly right."

Bob Fitzsimons and Tom Stritch were a year younger than Bruno Schlesinger, and so they grew old together, until Bob died in 1992. Each of them had a strong and distinctive personality, to be sure, but they also were mutually supportive, with unity in their faith and in their devotion to things of the mind. They were all three of them brilliant and innovative teachers, wholeheartedly dedicated to the well-being of their students. They reveled in one another's company They are gone now, and I miss them. It was my privilege to have known them.

Eulogy – Growing up a Son of Bruno Schlesinger

Tom Schlesinger[7]

September 22, 2010

Dad was born in the small town of Neunkirchin, Austria in 1911. Dad lived an amazingly long time; his first memory was the sky lit up from the bombing of a munitions factory during WWI. One of the darker parts of his life occurred when Hitler rose to power in Germany. Dad's pursuit of a law degree was interrupted by the Nazi occupation of Austria in 1938. He illegally crossed the border into France – as a child I had visions of the young Bruno, dressed in tweed like Sean Connery, escaping across the border. Unfortunately, he was arrested but did finally make it to America. His parents wrote letters for a while; we later learned they were sent to a concentration camp.

In the United States, he married Mom, whom he had known in Austria, now a struggling artist, who was to be his wife for seventy years. To survive he took a number of jobs that now seem incongruous with the professor that many of you came to love. He worked as a Fuller Brush man and a green grocer. He started a promising career as a hot dog vendor, but unfortunately the cart got washed away in a heavy rainstorm and with it his new career. Eventually he found his way to Notre Dame where he would earn a Ph.D in Political Science and come to teach at Saint Mary's.

For many American families, Sunday afternoon revolves around pro football. Its only fitting that a lot of our family life seemed centered around the campuses of Notre Dame/Saint Mary's. For some of you, you may remember Dad's slow, deliberate pace with his walker but I remember the years when Dad would take brisk evening walks around the lakes at Notre Dame.

---

7   Tom Schlesinger holds a Ph.D. in Political Science specializing in health care policy. He is an Executive Consultant at Gundersen Lutheran an integrated healthcare system. He has a wife and two children one just entering high school and the other attending Fordham University and considering a major in philosophy.

If we went out to eat as a family, it was usually to what we called "The Oak Room", otherwise known as the 'pay-caf' on the South Quad. After dinner, Dad would indulge himself in endless cups of coffee. Now that I think about it, I'm pretty sure he was not so much savoring the coffee as the opportunities to talk with the faculty that frequented the place. He seemed to thrive on these interactions with faculty and students.

As a father myself I know what a challenge it is to find family activities to bring us all together. Dad enjoyed his own unique version of Game Night. At our house Game Night consisted of a slide show of famous paintings and we the kids were called up to 'Name That Picture!' I actually thought I got pretty good.

One of my fondest memories was our time in Chicago after I had moved there. Dad would take the South Shore Line into town where he would always then visit his favorite bookstores and record stores. We would meet in the lobby of the Palmer House Hotel and enjoy a good German dinner at the Berghoff restaurant.

One year my sister Mary, Dad and I took a trip to Belgium and France together. Can you imagine how great it is to have 'Dr. Schlesinger' personally be your tour guide in Europe? It was a truly an amazing experience. Lucky for me I had been raised in the right environment of art and architecture and enjoyed all those days filled with churches and museums.

Those of you who knew Dad know that he loved to constantly learn about the world around him, primarily through book, magazines and newspapers. So it was a hard blow to him when macular degeneration eventually robbed him of his vision.

My first thought was to turn to the new software that reads aloud to the blind. Now I wasn't sure if I should reveal this tightly held family secret, but Dad was pretty much a Luddite when it came to the world of computers. So instead we hired graduate students to come in five days a week and read to him the New York Times.

I take enjoyment in knowing that Dad's love of reading has been passed down to my children. Every visit we made to South Bend included a trip to Barnes & Noble with Matthew and Mikaela. And believe it or not, they both looked forward to their trips there, knowing that grandpa would buy them hot chocolate and the book of their choice.

While Mom has wanted to move to Santa Barbara for 20 years, Dad was terribly reluctant to leave his roots here in South Bend. But, when he learned that Mom would not live much longer, he chose to let go of all the security that he knew for over 60 years, and at age 99, move to California.

So it was in the spring of this year, Dad finally agreed it was time for them to move closer to family; my sister Mary and brother John lived nearby in Santa Barbara.

Just a couple of months after they arrived in Santa Barbara, Dad suffered a serious fall and suffered a serious fracture. Complications from this break led to a rapid decline. Two weeks after the break he was admitted to hospice. You know he was never terribly comfortable in English, and in his last week of life he actually reverted to German. When I asked him, in German, to speak English, Dad told me that I should know German.

In the last few days he neither spoke nor acknowledged us. Yet it was so touching, Mom would ask to be wheeled into his room to hold his hand or read to him – just as he had done for her. At one point Mom asked us to help her up so she could give Dad a kiss, and she swears that he turned his head and returned his kiss. They truly shared a special bond that became more evident in the past few years.

Throughout his life Dad had a great love for classical music and opera. In his closing days he listened to his favorites for hour after hour. He passed away peacefully at his apartment, as he had requested, surrounded by his family.

Dad truly loved being a teacher and keeping up with the lives of his former students. His love of learning and witty sense of humor is still alive in us all.

Thank you all for coming tonight. Mom would have loved to be here but she is quite frail. Yet to you all, she sends her best wishes. Thank you.

Responses to Dawson's Ideas In the United States

Bruno Schlesinger

First published in The Chesterton Review
1985

BRUNO SCHLESINGER is Chairman of the Humanistic Studies Program at Saint Mary's College, Notre Dame, Indiana.

Christopher Dawson's ideas on Christian culture stimulated considerable discussions. Between 1953 and 1961, numerous articles, replies, and rejoinders to replies, appeared in such journals as *America, Commonweal, Thought, Catholic World, Perspectives* and *Educational Record*. In 1955, The University of Notre Dame arranged a conference of Deans of Catholic liberal arts colleges on the theme of Christian Culture. A symposium on Dawson's proposals, organized by Mr. John J. Mulloy, was held at Rosemont College and Villanova University in 1959. Professor Dawson attended this meeting and participated in a lively discussion.

A considerable number of prominent Catholic intellectuals lent Dawson's plans vigorous support. To mention a few names, still familiar to us today: John Courtney Murray, S.J., Thomas Merton, Leo Ward, Monsignor J.C. Ellis, and Frank Sheed.

In an assessment of Dawson's ideas, Murray wrote:

> I believe strongly that the theme of Christian culture ought to be a theme of Christian education and that it ought to be dealt with both historically and analytically— and, quite obviously, comparatively. Two advantages are clear: first, the acquisition of a sense of the civilisational heritage that men of the Church did so much to amass; and second, the cultivation of standards in terms of which to adopt a stance, both critical and sympathetic, in the face of the full l contemporary cultural situation.

I believe, as one must, in the principle of the renascence—the "critical return" to the past, the seizure in the past of the truly creative principles, and their adaptation under the altered circumstances of the moment. The study of Christian culture, as you have outlined it, ought to serve well for the preparation of students who may be instruments of some manner of Christian renascence.

I was particularly impressed by the stress you lay on the study of sources—certain great documents of the Tradition, as well as documents that have served to fashion the "counter-position." This is fine. There must always be a resourcement [sic].[8]

The brilliant Protestant theologian, Jarosłav Pelikan, wrote:

I am sure that only through such a study as this can American Christians recover their sense of belonging to something older and deeper than they themselves or their country are. Although this is a problem for American Protestants in a special way, American Roman Catholics, too, tend either to reject tradition for the wrong reasons or to exalt the wrong traditions. It is by exchanging their recent and shallow traditions for the substance of the Tradition that they can belong once more to the Christian community of discourse.[9]

On the other hand, a sizeable group of educators and administrators opposed Dawson. Although they approached the "eminent English Catholic historian" with almost excessive deference, they cared much less for his role as a latter-day reformer of Catholic higher education. Some of the charges were that he had not been able to "reduce his plans to manageable form" or that "educational blueprints were not Mr. Dawson's specialty." The Reverend Richard Rousseau, S.J., termed Dawson's project a solution of "despair": by permitting only Christian themes, he was

---

8 Personal Communication, February 26, 1961.
9 Personal Communication, March 14, 1961.

"crushing out all else."[10] When Dawson, with great patience, attempted to correct some gross misreadings, he elicited further irony about the "piecemeal revelation of exactly what the Christian culture proposal means."

The fact that an English writer offered critical suggestions to American colleges, added another bit of tension. "American educators," Helene Margaret complained, were "too sensitive to their imperfections. If Mr. Dawson finds them wanting, they agree."[11] In any case, according to her, the achievements of Catholic colleges in teaching Christian culture were overlooked. What most critics seemed to agree on was that there was *no need* for major changes of the curriculum. Dawson's intentions, argued Reverend Robert Hartnett, S.J. (then Editor-in-Chief of *America*) were to counteract contemporary secularisation. But secularisation was a European disease; Dawson's views did not apply to the United States. If there were any inroads of secularism in America, they had been arrested by Catholic educators.

Hartnett wrote:

> "By and large, we have kept the channels for the transmission of Christian culture fairly wide open and are in the process of opening them wider all the time."[12]

When all was said and done, Father Hartnett could not envisage what role the study of Christian culture could play in the American Catholic College.

More than anything else, however, it was the predominant position of philosophy and theology in the curriculum which blocked any major revision such as the study of Christian culture entailed. From the 1920's on, a large number of required courses in Thomist philosophy and theology formed the core of the Catholic college curriculum, giving it intellectual form and content. The concordance of philosophy and theology, linking speculation on a supernatural level with rational discourse, appeared as an ideal form of curriculum integration. Moreover, the "scholastic synthesis" received enthusiastic backing from the teaching clergy, who by training and inclination were more attuned to the abstract, logical,

---

10 Richard Rousseau, S.J., in Perspectives, Volume 5, p. 25.
11 Helene Margaret, in America, Volume 91, p. 542.
12 Robert Hartnett, S.J., in America, Volume 93. p. 76.

scholastic approach than to the more tentative, "concretising" historical method.

Some critics, products and advocates of Scholasticism, were probably not sufficiently prepared to pass judgment on Dawson's proposals; yet they rejected them, if only to ward off a potential threat to the established curriculum. Professor James Mullaney called attention to the danger of "cultural relativism" implicit in Dawson's ideas; according to Mullaney, systematic courses in theology and philosophy were needed to check that threat[13].

More forceful was the influential Dean of the Catholic University, Reverend James M. Campbell, when he called on his fellow educators to establish a favorable setting for theology and philosophy "to exercise the function as the integrating core of the liberal-arts curriculum." Although he conceded that Dawson had discovered an "enormous lacuna," Campbell assigned to Christian culture only an "ancillary role, geared to the master-disciplines of philosophy and theology."[14]

As one expected, the armies of Scholasticism remained victorious in the battle of the books: only one college. Saint Mary's, Notre Dame, under its President, Sister Madaleva, adopted Dawson's ideas: in 1956, a Christian Culture Program, organized as an interdisciplinary major, was started at Saint Mary's. The fledgling course profited greatly from much advice and encouragement generously offered by Professor Dawson. Over a period of twenty-five years, the Program attracted many students who found its offerings intellectually stimulating and rewarding.[15]

In a strange turn of events, the scholastic synthesis crumbled and collapsed in the sixties. Decline and fall occurred with amazing speed; no full explanation of the reasons why has been offered yet. But the celebrated scholastic core presented formidable problems at the very outset; aside from the efforts of a few masterful teachers, the vast, intricate web of Thomism resisted all attempts to scale it down to the undergraduate level.

A prominent Catholic philosopher, Germain Grisez, described the situation in philosophy:

> The systematic courses in philosophy were for the most part a rationalistic version of Thomism which

---

13 James Mullaney, in Commonweal, Volume 59, p. 381.

14 James M. Campbell, in America, Volume 93, p. 74.

15 The Course was renamed "Humanistic Studies" in order to avoid constant confusion with the Theology major.

St. Thomas would not have recognized. Textbooks, which were often uniform for an entire department, were English-language versions of earlier Latin seminary manuals.[16]

And on the teaching of Theology, Grisez wrote:

"Intellectual quest for understanding of faith was displayed by unreflective inculcation of religious information, with an intellectually inadequate apologetics much emphasized."[17]

The demise of the scholastic synthesis has confronted educators with grave, vexing questions concerning the "Catholic identity." Some educators seem to have simply surrendered to the prevailing spirit of secularism.

There are hardly any spokesmen for the Christian culture experiment left on the present scene, but Dawson's influence has not entirely vanished. Some of the new programs offered by American and Canadian colleges bear the unmistakable imprint of Dawson's ideas, although, strangely enough, his name appears nowhere in any of the course announcements. Possibly, some colleges assume that Dawson's books come from so far back in time that they have virtually become part of the public domain. Besides, up-to-date curriculum designers know better than to acknowledge a debt to Christopher Dawson: an academic program stands a far better chance of gaining grants and prestige if it is presented as fresh, home-grown and innovative.

---

16 Germain Grisez, in Why Should the Catholic University Survive?, ed. G.A. Kelly (New York, 1973), p. 43.

17 Germain Grisez, in Why Should the Catholic University Survive?, ed. G.A. Kelly, p. 44.

Letter to Bruno P. Schlesinger, 1961

Thomas Merton[18]

from *Hidden Ground of Love,* William H. Shannon, *editor*

Editor's Note:

Prof. Schlesinger, in seeking comments and evaluations by various educators and scholars of the Christian Culture Program, wrote to Thomas Merton in 1961.

This is the reply from Merton, who at the time was very actively corresponding with a wide variety of intellectuals and policymakers, chiefly concerning modern Christianity, the Cold War and the existential threat of annihilation with atomic weapons (note a mention of *fallout lettuce*).

Merton's letter to Dr. Schlesinger, referred to as **Cold War Letter #8**, collected in *Hidden Ground of Love: Letters on Religious Experience & Social Concerns*, 1985, reflects some of the urgency of the period.

---

18 Thomas Merton (1915-1968) was a writer and Trappist monk at Our Lady of Gethsemani Abbey in Kentucky. His writings include such classics as *The Seven Storey Mountain, New Seeds of Contemplation*, and *Zen and the Birds of Appetite*. Merton is the author of more than seventy books that include poetry, personal journals, collections of letters, social criticism, and writings on peace, justice, and ecumenism.

December 13, 1961

I have taken a little time to get around to your letter of November 10th about the program for Christian Culture at St. Mary's. This is a very important question and I am afraid I will not entirely do justice to it, but at least I can set down a few thoughts that occur to me, and hope for the best.

Thomas Merton

First of all, the urgent need for Christian humanism. I stress the word "humanism," perhaps running the risk of creating wrong impressions. What is important is the fully Christian notion of man: a notion radically modified by the mystery of Incarnation. This I think is the very heart of the matter. And therefore it seems to me that a program of Christian culture needs to be rooted in the biblical notion of man as the object of divine mercy, of a special concern on the part of God, as the spouse of God, as, in some mysterious sense, an epiphany of the divine wisdom. Man in Christ. The New Adam, presupposing the Old Adam, presupposing the old paradise and the new paradise, the creation and the new creation.

At the present time man has ceased entirely to be seen as any of these. The whole Christian notion of man has turned inside out, instead of paradise we have Auschwitz. But note that the men who went into the ovens at Auschwitz were still the same elect race, the object of divine predilection...

These perspectives are shattering, and they are vital for Christian culture. For then in the study of Europe and European Christianity, Latin Christianity, we come up against a dialectic of fidelity and betrayal, understanding and blindness. That we have come to a certain kind of "end" of the development of Western Christianity is no accident, nor yet is it entirely the responsibility of

95

Christian culture, for Christian culture has precisely saved all that could be saved.

Yet was this enough? These are terrible problems and I am sure no one can answer.

In a word, perhaps we might profitably run the risk, at least those who are thinking about the course behind the scenes, not just assuming that Christian culture is a body of perfections to be salvaged but of asking where there was infidelity and imperfection. And yet at the same time stressing above all the value and the supreme importance of our Western Christian cultural heritage.

For it is the survival of religion as an abstract formality without a humanist matrix, religion apart from man and almost in some sense apart from God Himself (God figuring only as Lawgiver not as Saviour), religion without any kind of human epiphany in art, in work, in social forms: this is what is killing religion in our midst today, not the atheists. So that one who seeks God without culture and without humanism tends inevitably to promote a religion that is irreligious and even unconsciously atheistic.

It would seem that the a-cultural philistinism of our society were the preferred instrument of demonic forces to finally eviscerate all that is left of Christian humanism.

I am thinking of an appalling item read in our refectory yesterday in which we were informed that at last religion was going to be put on the map in America by the "advertising industry". Here with the sublimely cynical complacency we were informed that now everybody would be urged in the most shallow, importunate, tasteless and meaningless ways, that they had to go to some church or synagogue or conventicle of some sect. Just get to the nearest damned conventicle as fast as your legs can carry you, brother, and get on your knees and worship; we don't give a hoot how you do it or why you do it, but you got to get in there and worship, brother, because the advertising industry says so and it is written right here on the napkin in the place where eat your *fallout lettuce sandwich*.

Sorry if I sound like a beatnik, but this is what is driving intelligent people as far from Christianity as they can travel.

Hence, in one word, a pretended Christianity, without the human and cultural dimensions which nature herself has provided, in history, in social tradition, etc., our religion becomes a lunar landscape of meaningless gestures and observances. A false supernaturalism which theoretically admits that grace builds on nature and then proceeds to eliminate everything natural, there you have the result of forgetting our cultural and humanistic tradition.

To my mind it is very important that this experiment is being conducted in a Catholic women's college. This is to me a hopeful sign. I think women are perhaps capable of salvaging something of humanity in our world today. Certainly they have a better chance of grasping and understanding and preserving a sense of Christian culture.

And of course I think the wisdom of Sister Madeleva has a lot to do with the effectiveness of this experiment and its future possibilities. The word "wisdom" is another key word, I suspect. We are all concerned not just with culture but with wisdom, above all.

Here I might mention someone who I think ought to be known and consulted as a choragus for our music, and that is Clement of Alexandria. In fact I think one might profitably concentrate a great deal of attention on the Alexandrian school, not only the Christians, but all that extraordinary complex of trends, the Jewish and gnostic and neo-Platonist, Philo above all, and then the Desert Fathers too, just outside. And Origen of Alexandria. And the Palestinians who reacted against Alexandria, and the Antiochians. Here we have a crucially important seedbed of future developments...

But the whole question of Christian culture is a matter of wisdom more than of culture.

For wisdom is the full epiphany of God the Logos, or Tao, in man and the world of which man is a little exemplar. Wisdom does not reveal herself until man is seen as microcosm, and the whole world is seen in relation to the measure of man. It is this measure which is essential to Christian culture, and whatever we say or read, it must always be remembered.

I could develop this more, but have no time. I could refer you to a booklet that is being printed in a limited edition by Victor Hammer on this. I will ask him if perhaps he would consent to send the college a copy... The booklet is my Hagia Sophia, which might or might not have something to say (wisdom) that could be relevant. I hope I don't sound commercial, but probably do, alas.

Mark Van Doren was here talking about liberal education recently. He would be a good man to consult. He stresses the point that the liberal education is that which frees an (adult) mind from the automatism and compulsions of a sensual outlook.

Here again we rejoin the Alexandrians and Greeks. The purpose of a Christian humanism should be to liberate man from mere status of *animalis homo* to at least the level of *rationalis* and better still spiritual, gnostic or pneumatic.

But I have gone far enough for this time. If you have any questions, reflections or criticisms, they might stimulate another outburst one of these days... TM

•   •   •

Bruno P. Schlesinger, 1911 - 2010

Acknowledgments

From Vienna to South Bend: A Refugee Professor's Story
by Philip Gleason
Appeared first in <u>American Catholic Studies,</u> vol. 124, No. 2 (Summer 2013), pp. 71-85, and is reprinted here, with minor stylistic changes, and with the permission of the editors.

Photographs generously made available by **Mary Schlesinger** with permission of the Schlesinger family. Without her work, this project would not have been possible.

Additional photographs generously made available by **John Kovach**, Archivist at St. Mary's College.

Courier articles made available by the generous permission of St. Mary's College and Shannon Rooney, Editor-in-Chief of **Courier.**

A Talk with Professor Bruno Schlesinger by the late Nancy Fallon is used here with the generous permission of Prof. Steven M. Fallon.

Bruno's Song is copyright of Mary Griffin Burns. It is used here by generous permission.

Bruno Schlesinger: Father of My Mind is copyright of Patricia Ferris McGinn and is used here by her her generous permission.

Reflections on Bruno Schlesinger is copyright of Prof. Gail Mandell and is made available by her generous permission.

Bruno Schlesinger Among Friends is copyright of Prof. Marvin O'Connell and is used here with the generous permission of Prof. O'Connell.

Eulogy – Growing up a son of Bruno Schlesinger is copyright of Tom Schlesinger and is generously provided for this volume with his permission.

Response to Dawson's Ideas in the United States first appeared in The Chesterton Review and is used here with the generous permission of Fr. Ian Boyd, C.S.B., President of The G.K. Chesterton Institute for Faith & Culture

"To Bruno P. Schlesinger" from THE HIDDEN GROUND OF LOVE: THE LETTERS OF THOMAS MERTON ON RELIGIOUS EXPERIENCE AND SOCIAL CONCERNS by Thomas Merton, edited by William H. Shannon. Copyright © 1985 by the Merton Legacy Trust.
Reprinted by permission of Farrar, Straus and Giroux, LLC

Rick Regan is a writer and publisher based in Raleigh, NC. He is the author of several volumes of plays, poetry and a novel. He has a degree in English from The Catholic University of America.